Feb 23 2019

# GENES & GENETICS

# THE SCIENCE OF THE HUMAN BODY

# BODY SYSTEMS

# CELLS, TISSUES & ORGANS

# DISEASES

# EPIDEMICS & PANDEMICS

# GENES & GENETICS

# IMMUNOLOGY

**MASON CREST**
450 Parkway Drive, Suite D, Broomall, Pennsylvania 19008
(866) MCP-BOOK (toll-free)

James Shoals

First printing
9 8 7 6 5 4 3 2 1

ISBN (hardback) 978-1-4222-4195-0
ISBN (series) 978-1-4222-4191-2
ISBN (ebook) 978-1-4222-7614-3

Cataloging-in-Publication Data on file with the Library of Congress

Developed and Produced by National Highlights Inc.
Interior and cover design: Torque Advertising + Design
Production: Michelle Luke

# THE SCIENCE OF THE HUMAN BODY

# GENES & GENETICS

## JAMES SHOALS

**MASON CREST**

# KEY ICONS TO LOOK FOR:

 **Words to Understand:** These words with their easy-to-understand definitions will increase the reader's understanding of the text while building vocabulary skills.

 **Sidebars:** This boxed material within the main text allows readers to build knowledge, gain insights, explore possibilities, and broaden their perspectives by weaving together additional information to provide realistic and holistic perspectives.

 **Educational videos:** Readers can view videos by scanning our QR codes, providing them with additional educational content to supplement the text. Examples include news coverage, moments in history, speeches, iconic sports moments, and much more!

 **Text-Dependent Questions:** These questions send the reader back to the text for more careful attention to the evidence presented there.

 **Research Projects:** Readers are pointed toward areas of further inquiry connected to each chapter. Suggestions are provided for projects that encourage deeper research and analysis.

## QR CODES AND LINKS TO THIRD-PARTY CONTENT

You may gain access to certain third-party content ("Third-Party Sites") by scanning and using the QR Codes that appear in this publication (the "QR Codes"). We do not operate or control in any respect any information, products, or services on such Third-Party Sites linked to by us via the QR Codes included in this publication, and we assume no responsibility for any materials you may access using the QR Codes. Your use of the QR Codes may be subject to terms, limitations, or restrictions set forth in the applicable terms of use or otherwise established by the owners of the Third-Party Sites. Our linking to such Third-Party Sites via the QR Codes does not imply an endorsement or sponsorship of such Third-Party Sites or the information, products, or services offered on or through the Third-Party Sites, nor does it imply an endorsement or sponsorship of this publication by the owners of such Third-Party Sites.

# CONTENTS

# WHY DO WE LOOK LIKE OUR PARENTS?

Have you ever observed that many of our characteristics, such as eye color, hair color, height, and so on resemble our parents'? The transmission of characteristics from parents to offspring is known as heredity. We can easily expect that the wheat grains we sow will definitely grow into wheat plants, just as rats are produced only by rats.

## Genetics

Offspring is a product of sexual reproduction and therefore is generally **biparental** in origin. Though we are not exact replicas of our parents, we still possess variable degrees of resemblance with them.

## WORDS TO UNDERSTAND

**biparental:** describes an organism with two parents.

**gamete:** a mature haploid male or female germ cell that is able to unite with another of the opposite sex in sexual reproduction to form a zygote.

**meiosis:** a type of cell division.

**monoparental:** describes an organism that came from only one parent.

**replica:** an exact copy of something.

We also share resemblances with our brothers, sisters, and other family members. The traits that make us distinct individuals arise due to the phenomenon of variation. The branch of biology that deals with studies related to heredity is called genetics.

# Reproduction

One very important aspect of genetics is the mode of reproduction. There will be no variations between parents and offspring of a rose plant reproduced by cutting (asexual reproduction). However, a tomato plant reproduced by crossbreeding two parent plants (sexual reproduction) will display variations. In asexually reproducing organisms, the offspring is derived from a single parent and hence it is often referred to as **monoparental**. The offspring in such cases is an exact **replica** of its parents. Such offspring are known as clones. In plants, each individual clone is referred to as a ramet.

# Chromosomes

Genes are units of heredity; they are transmitted from generation to generation. They are located in the chromosomes and are made up of DNA (deoxyribonucleic acid), the molecule of inheritance. RNA (ribonucleic acid) also acts as a genetic information carrier in a few viruses where DNA is absent.

# Sexual Reproduction

In sexual reproduction the formation and fusion of two **gametes** is involved. **Meiosis** occurs prior to the formation of gametes, and it results in chance segregation and chance recombination of genes during the formation of an offspring. In other words, it generates variations. Thus, sexual reproduction adds variability in offspring during meiosis. If such variations accumulate on a very large scale in an offspring, they may result in formation of new species.

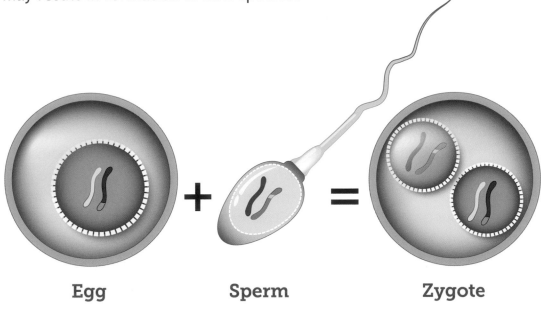

Egg    +    Sperm    =    Zygote

## SIDEBAR: DID YOU KNOW?

- The term *genetics* derives from the Greek word *genesis* (meaning descent), and was coined by William Bateson in 1906.

- A group of scientists kept some fruit flies in the dark for 57 years, or more than 1,400 generations. In time, the flies developed traits that enabled them to better function in darkness.

# EARLY THEORIES OF HEREDITY

The mystery of inheritance has intrigued people since ancient times. Many early philosophers and scientists tried to find out how traits passed from one generation to another. **Archaeologists** have found Babylonian clay tablets dating back to 6,000 years ago that recorded the **pedigrees** of horses and their desirable traits.

## Early Theories

One of the first theories of inheritance was proposed by Pythagoras, the great Greek philosopher and mathematician in the 6th century BC. He proposed that the bodies of animals released some kind of vapor, and that new individuals were formed from the combination of these vapors. Fast-forwarding to the 19th century, Charles Darwin proposed the theory of pangenesis. Darwin stated that the organs produced tiny heredity particles called gemmules. These particles migrated to the gametes and passed on the characteristics to the offspring. However, like most other ancient theories, this theory did not hold up.

## Why the Theories Failed

Most of these theories suggested that the characteristics of the parents get blended during transmission to the offspring, and therefore they

 **WORDS TO UNDERSTAND**

**chest cavity:** the cavity or hollow space in the chest enclosed by ribs between diaphragm and neck.

**mucus:** a thick fluid produced by some tissues that contains dead microorganisms

**pathogens:** infectious microbes capable of causing disease.

are often called theories of blending inheritance. There was, however, no practical and experimental proof for such theories of blending inheritance, and all of these were discarded. For example, the trait of sex never gets blended in the unisexual organisms; such individuals are either males or females. There is no mixing or "blending" of that characteristic.

Jean-Baptiste Lamarck

## Lamarck's Theory of Use and Disuse

In the early 1800s, Jean-Baptiste Lamarck, a French **naturalist**, proposed a theory known as the theory of use and disuse. It described how the structure of an organism altered over generations and how environment played an important role in that process. Lamarck proposed that by selective use and disuse of organs, organisms acquired

Original short-necked ancestor

Keeps stretching neck to reach leaves higher up on tree

and stretching until neck becomes progressively longer

Lamarck's theory

or lost certain traits during their lifetime. The use and disuse of organs was driven by the environment of the organism. The new traits were then passed on to their offspring, which led to a change in species over a period of time. This idea is also called the inheritance of acquired characteristics. For example, he said that present-day giraffes had longer necks because their ancestors had stretched to reach leaves higher up trees. This exertion caused their necks to grow longer, and that trait was inherited by their offspring. After many generations of neck stretching, the result was the present day long-necked giraffe.

Watch a video about heredity and family traits.

 SIDEBAR: DID YOU KNOW?

- The ancient Greek physician, Hippocrates, suggested that various body parts produced "seeds" that were transmitted to the offspring at the time of conception.
- An ancient school of thought, called Ovism, held that women carried eggs containing male and female children and that the sperm just stimulated the growth of the egg.

# MENDEL'S EXPERIMENTS

In the mid-1800s, the scientist and **friar** named Gregor Mendel observed the occurrence of two types of seeds in pea plants growing in the garden of the monastery where he lived. This made him interested in the study of **hybridization** experiments. He worked on seven pairs of varieties of garden pea (*Pisum sativum*). These varieties differed from each other in characteristics like plant height (tall/**dwarf**), flower position (axial/ terminal), pod shape (inflated/ constricted), pod color (green/yellow), seed shape (round/wrinkled), seed color (yellow/green), and seed coat color (gray/white). Ultimately, Mendel's work involved extensive hybridization experimentation with more than 10,000 pea plants.

Gregor Mendel

 **WORDS TO UNDERSTAND**

**dwarf:** describes an animal or plant that is smaller than is typical for that type.

**friar:** a member of a religious order, somewhat like a monk.

**hybridization:** a process in which a member of one plant or animal species is bred with a member of another, resulting in offspring that combine characteristics of both parents.

**postulate:** a proposition that is accepted as true in order to provide a basis for logical reasoning.

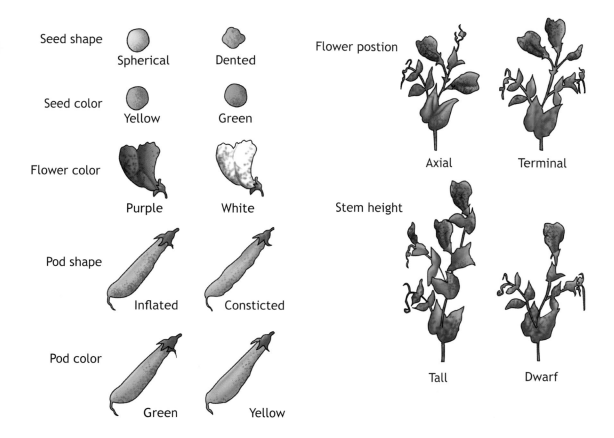

Seed shape — Spherical, Dented

Seed color — Yellow, Green

Flower color — Purple, White

Pod shape — Inflated, Consticted

Pod color — Green, Yellow

Flower postion — Axial, Terminal

Stem height — Tall, Dwarf

His findings, titled "Experiments on Plant Hybridization," were published in 1866. Out of four **postulates** (principle of paired factors, principle of dominance and recessiveness, principle of segregation of gametes, principle of independent assortment), the third, on segregation, proves to be universal even today. But despite this, the importance of Mendel's work was not immediately understood.

# Mendel's Factors

Most early theories were just assumptions. Mendel was the first to demonstrate the phenomenon of transmission of characteristics in a practical form. He was the first to declare that heredity is controlled by particles called germinal units or factors. He also stated that these factors were present in all cells and were transmitted from one generation to other through germ cells (gametes).

# Rediscovery of Mendel

It was in 1900 that Mendel's laws were rediscovered by three different scientists from different countries. They were Hugo de Vries (Holland), Carl Correns (Germany) and Erich von Tschermak (Austria). The pioneering work of Mendel was highly important, and its impact was so deep that after his findings the world of genetics was divided into two eras: Mendelian genetics and post-Mendelian genetics, regarding the progress made after him in this field.

## SIDEBAR: DID YOU KNOW?

- Carl Correns raised the status of two of Mendel's generalizations to the level of Laws.
- The factors of Mendel are now called genes. The term gene was coined by Wilhelm Johannsen (1909).

# DARWIN & EVOLUTION

Charles Robert Darwin was born on February 12, 1809—coincidentally, the exact same day and year as Abraham Lincoln's birthday. The young Darwin was an ordinary child and his childhood passed uneventfully. But later, after the five-year voyage of the HMS *Beagle*, Darwin made history. He worked very hard during those years collecting animal and plant materials, **geological** samples of interest, and even fossils. When he returned, he changed the way we think about living things.

## Darwin's Idea

Darwin developed an idea that can explain the past and predict the future of life on the earth. He put forward the theory of **evolution**. A species is a group of living organisms that are very similar to each other and share many similar characteristics. For example, all roses belong to one species, as do all dogs. Individuals of one species can mate with individuals of their own species, but not with those belonging to other species.

Charles Darwin

 **WORDS TO UNDERSTAND**

**evolution:** the process by which living things progress and transform, developing new variations.

**geological:** relating to the study of Earth's physical structure.

**scarcity:** shortage of something.

HMS *Beagle* at Tierra del Fuego (painted by Conrad Martens), from *The Illustrated Origin of Species* by Charles Darwin

# Survival of the Fittest

Darwin noted that some animals and plants produce large numbers of offspring. For instance, you might see many tadpoles at the start of spring, but only a few frogs during the rainy season. This is because a lot of them die due to food **scarcity**. They all try their best to get the required food for their growth and development, and in this process they even have to compete with each other. Darwin realized that all the members of a species are unique, they are all slightly different. Such important observations of Darwin lead him to publish a book called *On the Origin of Species by Means of Natural Selection* in 1859.

# Natural Selection

Darwin's theory of evolution stresses the point that evolution is a slow, gradual process. Complex creatures evolve from simplistic ancestors naturally over time. The main features of the theory of natural selection are:

- All living organisms tend to multiply. Insects lay hundreds of eggs and plants produce thousands of seeds for this purpose.
- In spite of rapid multiplication of different species, food and space are limited. So when the space and natural resources tend to contract, there will be competition amongst the members of different species as well as members of same species. This is called the "struggle of existence."
- In this struggle, only the most fit individuals will survive.
- Only these fit survivors will reproduce and transmit their genes to the next generation.

## SIDEBAR: DID YOU KNOW?

- **Darwin was only 22 years old when the HMS *Beagle* sailed off to make history.**

- **Though *Origin of Species* is Darwin's most popular book, he also wrote many other books, including *The Structure and Distribution of Coral Reefs* (1842), *Journal of Researches into the Natural History and Geology of the Countries Visited During the Voyage of HMS Beagle* (1845), and *The Descent of Man* (1872).**

# CHROMOSOMES

We now know that the traits are transmitted from one generation to next as discrete particulate units known as genes. A highly coordinated process works in an orderly manner in all sexually reproducing organisms to maintain genetic continuity. Genes cannot move from one cell to another or from one generation to another by themselves. The structure that serves as their vehicle of transmission is known as a chromosome. Genes segregate during meiosis and recombine after fertilization in a zygote.

## WORDS TO UNDERSTAND

**allosome:** a chromosome that differs from an ordinary chromosome in form, size, or behavior.

**cytoplasm:** the material within a living cell, excluding the nucleus.

**eukaryote:** organism made up of cells that possess a membrane-bound nucleus.

**nucleus:** a membrane-bound structure that contains the cell's hereditary and growth and reproduction information.

## Number and Shape

The number of chromosomes is constant for each species. For example, all human beings possess 46 chromosomes in their body cells. Generally, the chromosomes of animals are smaller than those of plants. There is a narrow area somewhere along the length of a chromosome, which is called a centromere. Chromosomes may look rod-shaped (or I-shaped), J-shaped, or V-shaped.

## Sex Chromosomes

Some chromosomes are also responsible for determining the sex of an organism; we call them sex chromosomes. In humans the diploid chromosome number is 46 (23 pairs). Twenty-two pairs are called autosomes, and the 23rd pair is that of the sex chromosome (**allosome**). The members of this 23rd pair are identical (XX) in females and different (XY) in males.

## DNA

The main component of chromosomes is DNA, which stores genetic information in the form of genes.
DNA supplies the information necessary for cells to function. Nucleic acids (DNA and occasionally RNA) constitute the genetic material of all living organisms. The facts that DNA is present in all cells, is capable of replication, of controlling the cell structure and functions, and of undergoing mutations, are responsible for designating it as the molecule of inheritance.

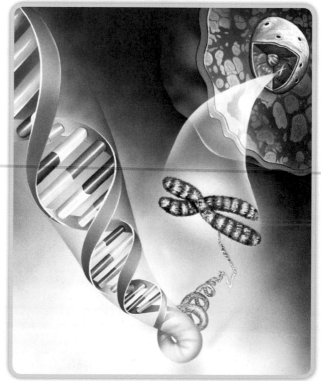

# Eukaryotic and Prokaryotic Chromosomes

In **eukaryotes** the chromosomes are well-organized structures and lie inside the **nucleus**. On the other hand, the prokaryotes possess a single molecule of DNA that lies naked inside the **cytoplasm**; it is known as nucleiod or prochromosome. Eukaryotic chromosomes are highly condensed structures because of the presence of some specific proteins called histones. Whereas the chromosomal DNA is in circular form in prokaryotes, it is linear in eukaryotes.

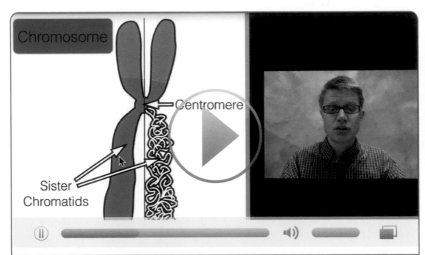

**Watch a video about chromosomes.**

## SIDEBAR: DID YOU KNOW?

- Chromosomes attain very large shapes in certain animal and plant cells. Polytene chromosomes found in salivary glands of fly larvae, and lampbrush chromosomes in the oocytes of many vertebrates and some invertebrates are examples of such giant chromosomes.

- The adder's tongue fern (*Ophioglossum reticulatum*) possesses the largest chromosome number. Its diploid (2n) chromosome number is 1,262.

# GENES & ALLELES

You might have heard some person saying, "It's in my genes." He might have been talking about the resemblances (physical appearance, intelligence, etc.) he shares with other members of his family. It is well-known that genes play an important role in shaping our overall body functioning and personality. Genes are made up of DNA and are carried on the chromosomes from one cell to other and from one generation to next.

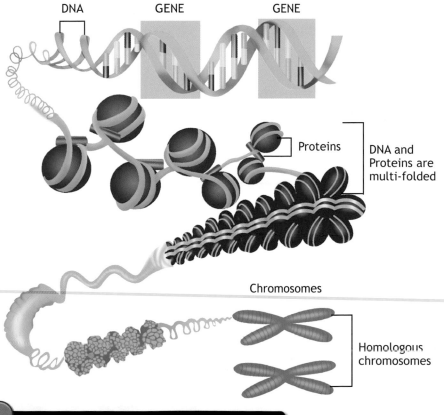

DNA  GENE  GENE

Proteins

DNA and Proteins are multi-folded

Chromosomes

Homologous chromosomes

## WORDS TO UNDERSTAND

**mutation:** any alteration in the genetic structure.
**spontaneously:** in an unplanned way.
**variant:** alternative or different from the norm.

# Importance of Genes

Genes are responsible for the determination of specific human traits like hair and eye color, height, blood group, etc. Since we receive one chromosome from each of our parents we possess two genes for one characteristic. They may be identical (XX) or different (XY), and therefore exhibit different expressions in different individuals. The expression of some characteristics is controlled by a single gene, whereas other characteristics are controlled by a combination of different genes. DNA is made up of four chemicals (A, T, G, and C), and their patterns are responsible for coding and manufacturing different chemicals that finally enable our body to grow, develop, and function. Genes therefore contain instructions for manufacturing proteins and enzymes. Whenever a cell divides, genes pass on to the daughter cells and hence the genetic information, too.

## Alleles

The exact place on the chromosome where a gene is located is known as the locus. The two genes that occur on the same locus in the two homologous chromosomes of an individual are called alleles. Interestingly,

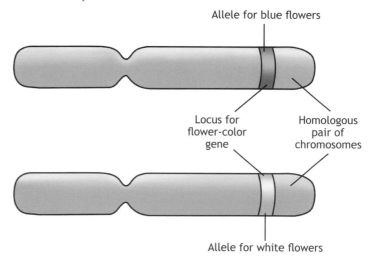

Allele for blue flowers

Locus for flower-color gene

Homologous pair of chromosomes

Allele for white flowers

both of these also control the expression of any single characteristic. So alleles are the genes that control two alternate forms of a single trait, for example, tallness and shortness in the case of stem height of Mendel's pea plant. Generally, there are two alleles for a given characteristic, but their number may be more than two at times. For example, in the case of our blood groups, we possess three alleles A, B, and i. But since we have only two chromosomes of one type, we can have only two of these alleles in our cells.

# Genetic Mutation

Sometimes there may be variations in the information contained in the genes; we call this gene **mutation**. Such changes occur **spontaneously** due to aging or are induced when cells get exposed to some chemicals or radiation. Most of the time cells can recognize these mutations and repair them. If not repaired such changes can cause illnesses, and moreover if the gene mutation occurs in gametes (egg or sperm), the offspring can inherit the mutated gene from their parents. Generally, people carry 5-10 variants or diseased genes in their cells. Some of the genes may even lead to the death of organism, and these are known as lethal genes. People who are concerned that they might carry certain **variant** genes do genetic testing so they can learn their children's risk of having a disease.

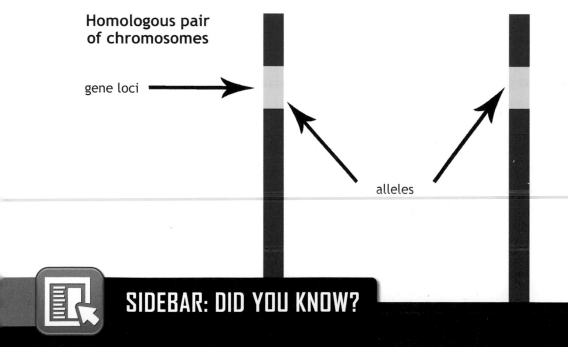

Homologous pair of chromosomes

gene loci

alleles

## SIDEBAR: DID YOU KNOW?

- If stretched out into a thread, the DNA in every cell in our bodies is nearly 6 feet long!
- Gene mutations are also known as point mutations.

# DOMINANCE & RECESSIVENESS

Try to recall Mendel's pea plant experiment. When a tall plant (TT) was crossed with a dwarf plant (tt), the **progeny** was only tall-stemmed. This means that the allele responsible for tallness (T) is not allowing its counterpart (t) to be expressed in heterozygous condition (Tt). So the allele of a dwarf stem (T) can express itself only in the absence of T; it can happen only when it is present in homozygous form (tt)

## Dominant and Recessive Genes

From Mendel's experiment, it became clear that genes can be dominant (T) or recessive (t). Dominant genes express their effect even if there is only one copy of that gene in the pair. They are considered to be of a wild type, and are usually widespread in the population. The recessive genes (t), on the other hand, are less common and are thought to have formed by mutation in the wild allele. These are therefore also known as mutant alleles.

## Homozygous and Heterozygous Individuals

A characteristic is represented in an organism (diploid) by two alleles of a same gene. The individual that contains identical alleles for a given characteristic in its homologous chromosomes are called homozygous. The homozygote is therefore always pure for a given trait. For example, if the condition is TT, it will be pure for tallness, and if the condition

 **WORDS TO UNDERSTAND**

**genotype:** the genetic constitution of an individual organism.
**hybrid:** an organism that is the offspring of genetically dissimilar parents.
**progeny:** offspring of animals or plants.

# How Genetic Diseases are Shared in Families

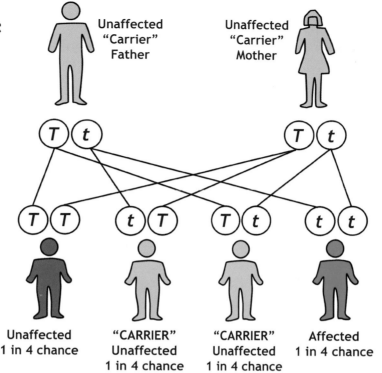

Unaffected "Carrier" Father

Unaffected "Carrier" Mother

Unaffected
1 in 4 chance

"CARRIER"
Unaffected
1 in 4 chance

"CARRIER"
Unaffected
1 in 4 chance

Affected
1 in 4 chance

is tt, it will be pure for dwarfism. However, if there is presence of two alternative forms of the gene (Tt), the individual will be called heterozygote. It will not be pure, and we call it a **hybrid**. When a heterozygote is crossed with its double recessive parent (Tt×tt), the process is called testcross.

# Incomplete Dominance

The alleles are not necessarily related as dominant and recessive. We have examples where two pure line parents breed to give an intermediate expression of the characteristic. In a Four O'Clock plant, when a pure line red (RR) parent make a cross with a pure line white (rr) parent, their progeny bears an intermediate flower color (pink). It means that the gene responsible for the red flower color cannot completely mask the expression of its allele. Such a condition is called incomplete dominance, blending inheritance, or intermediate inheritance.

# Codominance

We still have cases when both of the alleles interact in such a way that instead of making an intermediate expression, both equally express themselves in the hybrid individuals. Such a phenomenon is called codominance. There are two types of pure short-horned cattle, red and white. The hybrids of red and white individuals are found to have both colors, which is the juxtaposition of small patches of red and white. It means that there is no blending of characteristics here (as there was in incomplete dominance), but both the alleles are equally capable of expressing themselves. This type of inheritance is also known as mosaic inheritance. The allele for sickle cell hemoglobin (HbS) is codominant with its allele for normal hemoglobin (HbA).

## SIDEBAR: DID YOU KNOW?

- Each cross between a hybrid individual (Tt) and either of its parents (TT or tt) is called a reciprocal cross.

- The genetic constitution of an organism with regard to one or more characteristics is called its genotype. The phenotype, on the other hand, refers to the observable external characteristics.

# THE CELL CYCLE

New cells are formed by the division of preexisting cells. Cell division is the means of cell multiplication, and it maintains the continuity of living matter. In **unicellular** organisms, cell division is the basis of reproduction. As soon as the cell divides, it forms two new individuals. However, in most multicellular organisms, cell division is responsible for the formation of tissues, organs, organ systems, and the whole organism.

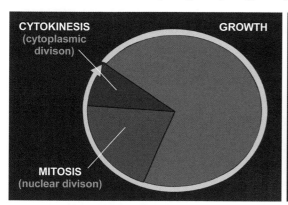 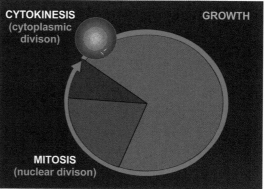

## The Cell Cycle

Daughter cells that are formed after the division of parent cell may grow in size and divide again. This period of time between two **successive** divisions is called generation time. This time may vary from a few minutes to a few days depending on cell type and its environmental conditions. The series of changes involving the growth and division of cells is called the cell cycle. The cell cycle consists of two stages: a long, nondividing growing phase (I phase, or interphase), and a short, dividing phase (M phase).

 **WORDS TO UNDERSTAND**

**synthesize:** to combine so as to form a new, complex product.
**unicellular:** one-celled.
**successive:** in a row.

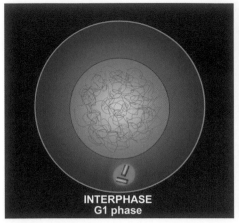

INTERPHASE
G1 phase

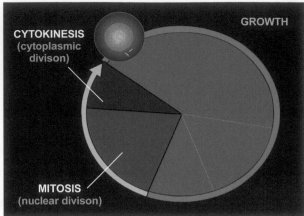

GROWTH

CYTOKINESIS
(cytoplasmic
divison)

MITOSIS
(nuclear divison)

# Interphase

Interphase constitutes a series of changes that takes place in the newly formed cell and nucleus before it becomes capable of division again. Earlier it was called the resting stage as there is no apparent activity related to cell division. But it is the time when a cell is metabolically quite active and prepares itself for division. There is replication of various subcellular components including chromosomes. The cell also grows in size. Interphase occupies about 70 to 90 percent of total generation time.

# Stages of Interphase

• **G1 phase**: the first growth phase. During this phase, RNA and proteins are **synthesized**. A large number of nucleotides are formed, and the cell organelles increase in number. The duration of this phase is variable. It is longer in cells that do not divide frequently and shorter in cells that undergo frequent divisions.

• **S phase**: the synthetic phase. During this time the chromosomes replicate. The DNA content doubles and a duplicate set of genes is formed. S-phase is also called invisible phase.

• **G2 phase**: the second growth phase. The formation of RNA and proteins continue during this phase. This is the time when the cell gets totally prepared for its division. It is followed by mitotic phase.

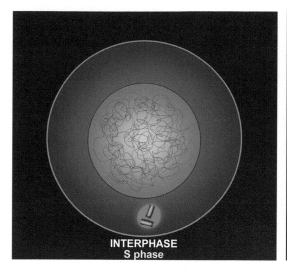

**INTERPHASE**
S phase

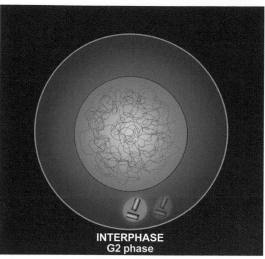

**INTERPHASE**
G2 phase

# CELL CYCLE

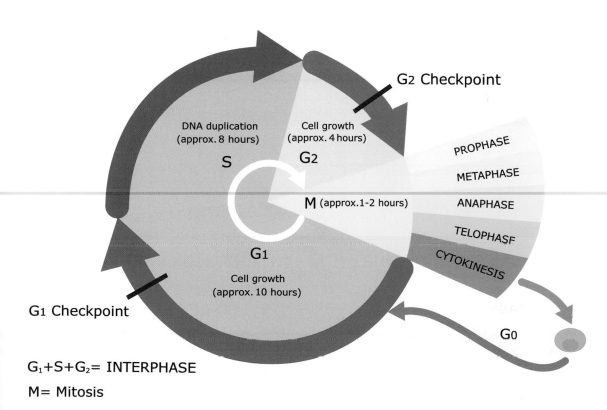

G2 Checkpoint

DNA duplication
(approx. 8 hours)

Cell growth
(approx. 4 hours)

S

G2

PROPHASE

METAPHASE

M (approx.1-2 hours)

ANAPHASE

TELOPHASE

CYTOKINESIS

G1

Cell growth
(approx. 10 hours)

G0

G1 Checkpoint

$G_1 + S + G_2 =$ INTERPHASE

M= Mitosis

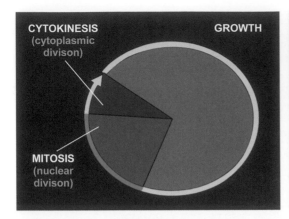

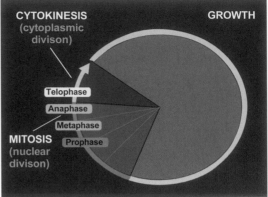

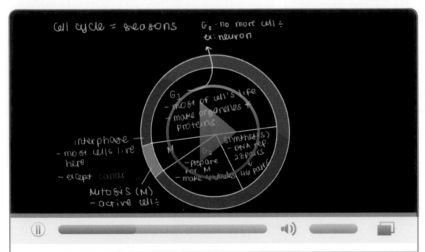

Watch a video
about the
cell cycle.

# SIDEBAR: DID YOU KNOW?

- The G1 phase of the cell cycle is called the checkpoint. Once it is crossed, the cell cycle will go on uninterrupted until it is completed.

- Rudolf Virchow was the first scientist to suggest that new cells are formed from the division of preexisting cells.

# CELL DIVISION

We now know that new cells arise from preexisting cells. A cell prepares itself for division during the interphase of the cell cycle. Immediately after G2 phase, the cell enters the division phase, also called the mitotic phase. So cell division is the process of formation of new cells (daughter cells) from the preexisting cell; it is also called cell reproduction or cell multiplication.

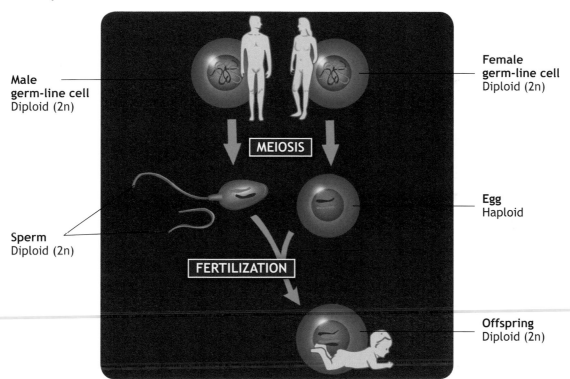

Male germ-line cell
Diploid (2n)

Female germ-line cell
Diploid (2n)

MEIOSIS

Sperm
Diploid (2n)

Egg
Haploid

FERTILIZATION

Offspring
Diploid (2n)

 **WORDS TO UNDERSTAND**

**amitosis:** direct cell division.

**degenerate:** decline in quality or purity.

**somatic cell:** any cell of a living organism other than the reproductive cells.

# Cell Division and Chromosome Number

We have two types of chromosome numbers. All body cells of an organism contain a definite number of chromosomes. This is called the diploid chromosome number and is written as 2n (for example, 2n=46 in humans). However, the number of chromosomes is reduced to half in germ cells (gametes) so that at the time of fertilization, the zygote can again have a 2n number identical to the parents. This chromosome number is known as the haploid chromosome number and is designated as n. Thus, n=23 in human beings.

# How Cells Divide

Cell division can occur in three ways: **amitosis**, mitosis, and meiosis. Out of these, amitosis, is the simplest method of cell reproduction. In this division there is no differentiation of chromosomes and the nuclear envelope does not **degenerate**. The nucleus simply elongates and constricts in the middle to form two daughter nuclei. This is then followed by cytoplasmic division. As compared to amitosis, other types of cell divisions (mitosis and meiosis) are known as indirect cell division.

# Mitosis

Mitosis is the type of cell division where the resultant daughter cells contain the equal number of chromosomes as the parent cell. In our **somatic cells** we have 46 chromosomes, and the daughter cells produced due to mitosis will also contain 46 chromosomes. This type of division is therefore also called equational division. Because mitosis occurs in the formation of somatic cells, it is also called somatic cell division.

# Stages of Mitosis

Mitosis consists of two steps. The stage when division of the nucleus occurs is called karyokinesis, and later, when the cytoplasm divides, it is called cytokinesis. Karyokinesis consists of four main stages: prophase, metaphase, anaphase, and telophase. Cytokinesis is, however, different in plants and animals. In an animal cell there is no rigid cell wall. Therefore, the cell develops a constriction in the center and divides into two; this is called cleavage cytokinesis. In plant cells, such constriction is not possible. The cell develops a plate in the center that then extends towards both sides of the cell wall. When this plate reaches both sides of the cell wall, the cell divides in to two; this method is called cell-plate method cytokinesis.

## Meiosis

Meiosis is the type of cell division where the resultant daughter cells contain half the number of chromosomes as the parent cell has. It is therefore also called reductional division. Meiosis occurs in the formation of germ cells (gametes), so in our germ cells we have 23 chromosomes only. In meiosis, we have two successive divisions: meiosis I and meiosis II. The first of these is the actual reductional division and therefore the number of chromosomes during Meiosis I get reduced to half. Meiosis II is identical to mitosis.

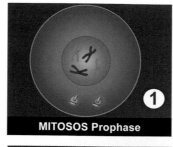
MITOSOS Prophase ①

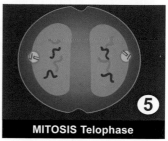
MITOSOS Telophase ④

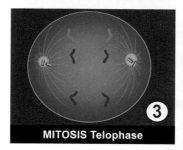
MITOSIS Anaphase ②

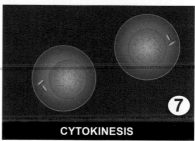
MITOSIS Telophase ⑤

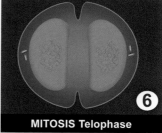
MITOSIS Telophase ③

MITOSIS Telophase ⑥

⑦
CYTOKINESIS

## SIDEBAR: DID YOU KNOW?

- Amitosis is also called direct cell division.
- In mitosis, a cell divides into two new cells but in meiosis it divides into four daughter cells.

# DEOXYRIBONUCLEIC ACID

Nucleic acids were first isolated by Friedrich Miescher from pus cells. We already know that the cell nucleus contains deoxyribose nucleic acid (DNA). DNA is present in all living creatures except some viruses. DNA is too small to see with the naked eye or even with a microscope. A more powerful method using X-rays must be used to see these tiny molecules.

## Storehouse of Genetic Information

DNA contains instructions that control the workings of cells in making the proteins which are the building blocks of all living organisms. DNA is somewhat like a cookbook. It is passed from parents to offspring and contains the instructions that enable the offspring to develop from a single cell into an adult body. The DNA is copied at the time of cell division.

## WORDS TO UNDERSTAND

**helix:** something with a shape like a corkscrew.
**nucleotide:** a compound that forms the base of nucleic acid.
**replicate:** copy or reproduce.

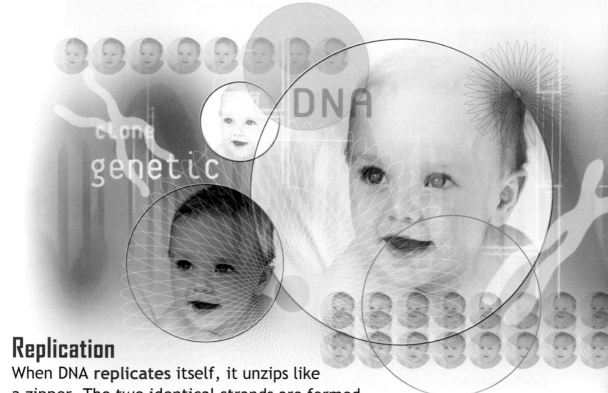

## Replication

When DNA **replicates** itself, it unzips like a zipper. The two identical strands are formed in front from the unzipped strands and two new DNA molecules are formed. It is then passed on from a one generation to other. That is why although an offspring resembles its parents, it is never identical because each offspring gets only some of the DNA each parent carries.

## Types of DNA

The DNA duplex model proposed by James Watson and Francis Crick is a right-handed spiral and is called B-DNA, and possessed 10 base pairs per turn. Other right-handed DNAs are A-DNA (11 base pairs per turn), C-DNA (nine base pairs per turn) and D-DNA (eight base pairs per turn). Z-DNA is the only left-handed double **helix** with a zigzag backbone; its one turn has 12 base pairs.

## Structure

The DNA molecule is shaped like a twisted ladder called a "double helix." The molecule is formed from subunits that consist of phosphate, sugar, and nitrogen bases. The side rails of the ladder are formed by the sugar phosphates, which is the backbone of DNA. There are also base pairs that are called bases. Bases are somehow the steps of the ladder. Each base has a name, but they are usually called by their initials: A, T, C, and G. A and T always pair up together—for example, as A-T—and C and G join up together—for example, C-G. The two strands of DNA fit in each other like a zipper.

Two of the **nucleotide** bases (A, G) are called purines and are double-ring structures. The remaining two (C, T) are single-ringed and are called pyrimidines. The total amount of purine nucleotides is always equal to the total amount of pyrimidine nucleotides. The proportion of A is equal to T, and that of C equal to G.

hydrogen-bonded bases

sugar phosphate backbone

 Adenine

Thymine

 Cytosine

 Guanine

# RIBONUCLEIC ACID

RNA gets its name from the sugar group in the molecule's backbone: ribose. RNA is the main genetic material in viruses. It is significant in the production of proteins in other living organisms. RNA can move around the cells of living organisms and thus serves as a sort of genetic messenger, relaying the information stored in the cell's DNA out from the nucleus to other parts of the cell where it is used to help make proteins.

## Similarities and Differences

Several important similarities and differences exist between RNA and DNA. Like DNA, RNA has a sugar-phosphate backbone with nucleotide bases attached to it. Like DNA, RNA contains the bases adenine (A), cytosine (C), and guanine (G); however, RNA does not contain thymine;

### Structure of DNA & RNA

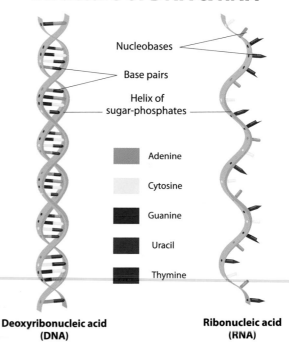

Nucleobases

Base pairs

Helix of sugar-phosphates

Adenine

Cytosine

Guanine

Uracil

Thymine

**Deoxyribonucleic acid (DNA)**

**Ribonucleic acid (RNA)**

## WORDS TO UNDERSTAND

**amino acid:** a type of organic acid which is the building block of proteins.

**biomolecule:** a molecule in living organisms, such as a protein.

**prokaryotes:** an organism made up of cells that lack a cell nucleus or any membrane-encased organelles.

instead, RNA's fourth nucleotide is the base uracil (U). Unlike the double-stranded DNA molecule, RNA is a single-stranded molecule. RNA molecules are smaller (shorter) than DNA molecules.

## Importance of RNA

RNA is needed to make proteins. In eukaryotes, RNA is synthesized from the DNA inside the nucleus and then it moves outside to the cytoplasm. In **prokaryotes**, as there is no nuclear membrane and the DNA lies naked in the cytoplasm, so the RNA and proteins are made in the cytoplasm itself.

## Functions of RNA

RNA is a very important **biomolecule**. In eukaryotes, since the master molecule (DNA) containing all information about synthesis of different proteins is sitting in the nucleus, and the protein factories (ribosomes) are situated in the cytoplasm, RNA is the only carrier of coded information from one place to other. RNA performs the functions of transmitting genetic information from DNA to proteins produced by the cell.

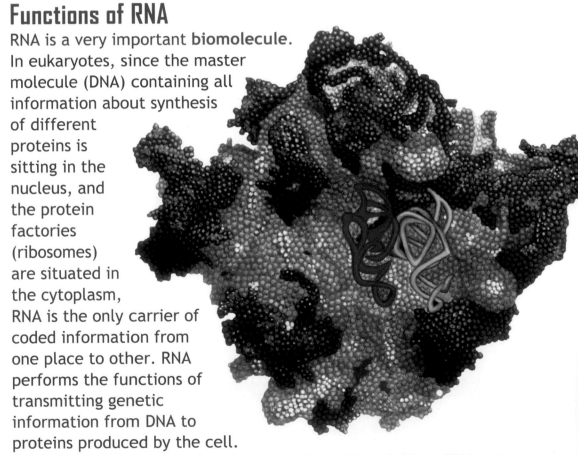

These are also concerned with monitoring cell activities. RNA acts as a special carrier molecule for **amino acids** to be used in protein synthesis.

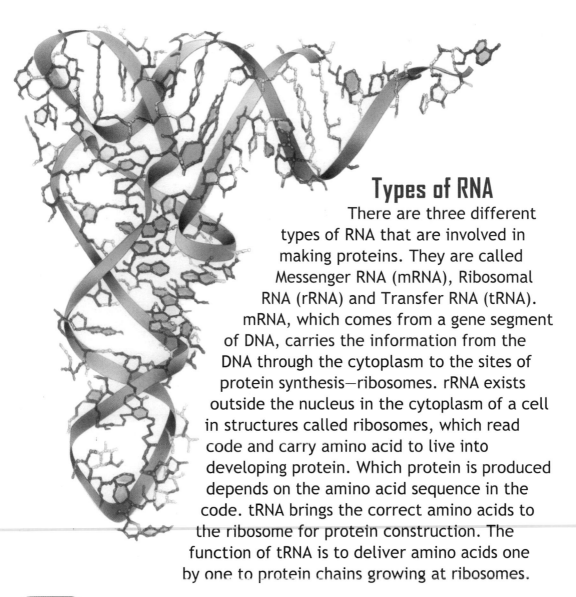

## Types of RNA

There are three different types of RNA that are involved in making proteins. They are called Messenger RNA (mRNA), Ribosomal RNA (rRNA) and Transfer RNA (tRNA). mRNA, which comes from a gene segment of DNA, carries the information from the DNA through the cytoplasm to the sites of protein synthesis—ribosomes. rRNA exists outside the nucleus in the cytoplasm of a cell in structures called ribosomes, which read code and carry amino acid to live into developing protein. Which protein is produced depends on the amino acid sequence in the code. tRNA brings the correct amino acids to the ribosome for protein construction. The function of tRNA is to deliver amino acids one by one to protein chains growing at ribosomes.

## SIDEBAR: DID YOU KNOW?

- tRNA (transfer RNA) is the smallest of all RNA molecules.
- RNA is synthesized from DNA by a process known as transcription.

# BLOOD GROUPS

Blood is an important component of our body that serves many functions. It consists of many types of cells floating around in **plasma** fluid. The red blood cells (RBCs) contain hemoglobin, a protein that binds oxygen. Therefore, RBCs are responsible for transporting oxygen to and removing carbon dioxide from, the body tissues. The white blood cells (WBCs) fight infection. The **platelets** help the blood to clot

## Different Blood Groups

The differences in our blood are due to the presence or absence of some protein molecules called antigens and antibodies. The antigens are located on the surface of the RBCs and the antibodies are in the blood plasma. Individuals have different types and combinations of these proteins. The blood group you belong to depends on what you have inherited from your parents.

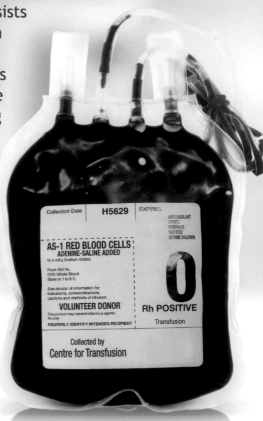

Collection Date    H5629    EXPIRES

ANTICOAGULANT
CITRATE
PHOSPHATE
DEXTROSE
ADENINE SOLUTION

**AS-1 RED BLOOD CELLS**
ADENINE-SALINE ADDED
15.4 mEq Sodium Added

From 450 mL
CPD Whole Blood
Store at 1 to 6 C.

See circular of information for
indications, contraindications,
cautions and methods of infusion.

**VOLUNTEER DONOR**
This product may transmit infectious agents.
Rx only
PROPERLY IDENTIFY INTENDED RECIPIENT

**Rh POSITIVE**
Transfusion

Collected by
**Centre for Transfusion**

## WORDS TO UNDERSTAND

**plasma:** the colorless fluid part of blood, lymph, or milk, in which corpuscles or fat globules are suspended.

**platelet:** a small, colorless disk-shaped cell fragment without a nucleus, found in large numbers in blood, and involved in clotting.

**toxic:** poisonous.

# What is Your Blood Group?

If your blood group is A, then you have A antigens on the surface of your RBCs and B antibodies in your blood plasma. If your blood group is B, then your RBC surfaces have B antigens and plasma contains A antibodies. In case of AB blood group, individuals have both A and B antigens on the surface of their RBCs, and no (A or B) antibodies in the blood plasma. Lastly, if you belong to the blood group O, you will have neither A or B antigens on the surface of your RBCs, but you will have both A and B antibodies in your blood plasma.

| | Group A | Group B | Group AB | Group O |
|---|---|---|---|---|
| Red blood cell type | A | B | AB | O |
| Antibodies present | Anti-B | Anti-A | None | Anti-A and Anti-B |
| Antigens present | A antigen | B antigen | A and B antigens | None |

# Rh Factor

There is also one more antigen on the surface of RBCs that is not present in all individuals. It is called Rh factor. Those who have it are called Rh+, and those who lack it are called Rh-. So if your RBCs possess antigen A on their surface, antibody B in your blood plasma, and also Rh factor, your blood group will be designated as A Rh+. If someone's RBCs possess antigen A and B on their surface, and no antibodies in the blood plasma, and the Rh factor is also absent, then his blood group will be designated as AB Rh-.

## Inheritance of Blood Groups

Inheritance is controlled by three alleles: A, B, and O. Where A and B are codominant, O is recessive to both of these. So, O blood group will be present when both of the alleles A and B are absent; the individual will have a genotype OO. On the other hand, when both A and B alleles are present, the blood group will neither A nor B, but AB.

## Blood Transfusions

Mixing blood from two individuals can lead to blood clumping. The clumped red cells can cause **toxic** reactions with fatal consequences. These clumps are formed due to the reaction between antigens and antibodies. Persons with blood group AB are universal recipients because they can receive blood from all groups, whereas individuals with blood group O can donate blood to all; they are therefore called universal donors.

# HUMAN CHROMOSOMES & CHROMOSOMAL DISORDERS

Human genetics is the branch of genetics that deals with the inheritance of characteristics in human beings. In 1901, Sir Archibald Garrod, a British physician, found that the innate defects of metabolism are controlled by genes and inherited in a Mendelian fashion. In 1956, Joe Hin Tijo and Albert Levan reputed their discovery that each cell of the human body contains 23 pairs of chromosomes—22 pairs of autosomes and one pair of sex chromosomes. The autosomes are similar in both males and females, but sex chromosomes are similar only in females (XX); they are dissimilar in males (XY).

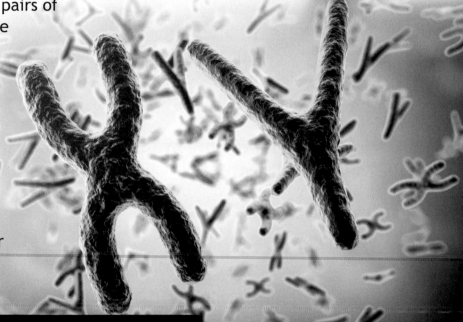

## WORDS TO UNDERSTAND

**anemia:** a condition caused by lack of red blood cells.

**Klinefelter's syndrome:** a syndrome affecting males in which the cells have an extra X chromosome (in addition to the normal XY).

**Turner's syndrome:** a syndrome affecting females in which an X chromosome is missing or damaged.

Therefore, a typical human female has 22 pairs of autosomes and one pair of sex (XX) chromosomes, and a typical human male has 22 pairs of autosomes and one pair of sex (XY) chromosomes. The Y chromosome is much smaller than the X chromosome.

## Sex Chromosomes

A female is always homozygous for the sex chromosome (XX); all the eggs therefore contain the X chromosome. Since the male is heterozygous (XY), he produces two types of sperm, either with gene X or gene Y. Therefore, the sex of the offspring depends on the type of sperm. If the egg (X always) is fertilized with sperm X, the offspring will be female, and when fertilized with sperm Y, the offspring is a male.

## Human Genetic Disorders

A change in the genetic makeup of an organism or an abnormality in a gene can lead to genetic disorders. A genetic disorder may or may not be inheritable. The following are a few genetic abnormalities in humans and their resultant disorders:

1. **Numerical abnormality in autosomes**: Down syndrome occurs due to numerical abnormality in autosomes. It is caused by the presence of an extra chromosome 21.

2. **Numerical abnormality in sex chromosome**: Alteration in the number of chromosomes is more common in sex chromosomes. In the case of **Klinefelter's syndrome**, the individual is a sterile male with XXY genotype. **Turner's syndrome** is caused by XO genotype. The affected individual is a sterile female with underdeveloped breasts and ovaries, and a small uterus.

Features of a child with down syndrome

# Sickle Cell Anemia

Sickle cell **anemia** is common in people of African descent, and those parts of the world where malaria is the major cause of death. In people suffering from sickle cell anemia, the red blood corpuscles attain a sickle-shaped structure. The change in the structure of red blood corpuscles occurs due to a defective type of hemoglobin called hemoglobin S. These sickle-shaped corpuscles do not live as long as normal red blood cells, and they can get stuck in blood capillaries, reducing blood circulation. Sickle cell anemia can be extremely painful.

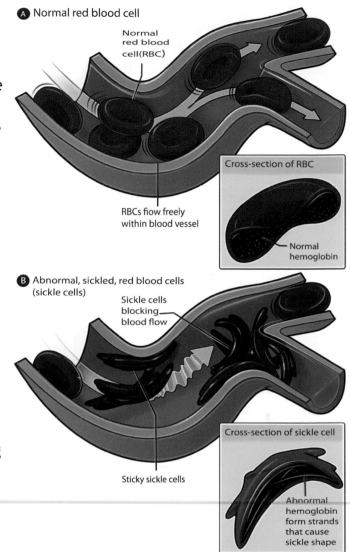

A Normal red blood cell

Normal red blood cell(RBC)

RBCs flow freely within blood vessel

Cross-section of RBC

Normal hemoglobin

B Abnormal, sickled, red blood cells (sickle cells)

Sickle cells blocking blood flow

Sticky sickle cells

Cross-section of sickle cell

Abnormal hemoglobin form strands that cause sickle shape

## SIDEBAR: DID YOU KNOW?

- Thalassaemias are a collection of genetic disorders involving reduced synthesis of red blood cells in bone marrow.

- Queen Victoria of England suffered from hemophilia, an inherited condition in which the blood doesn't clot well.

# GENETIC ENGINEERING

Suppose we have two different varieties of wheat plants: one that results in high yields but is **susceptible** to some diseases (variety 1), and the other with a very low yield but resistant to diseases (variety 2). If we isolate the gene responsible for disease resistance from variety 2 and introduce the same into the genome of variety 1, we can develop a new variety (variety 3), which will be better in yield and also disease resistant. These types of modifications are done using the different techniques of genetic engineering.

## WORDS TO UNDERSTAND

**diabetes:** a condition that impairs the body's ability to use food as energy.

**susceptible:** Likely or liable to be influenced or harmed by a particular thing.

**transgenic:** an organism that has had genes from another organism put into its genome.

# Applications of Genetic Engineering

Genetic engineering has a wide range of applications in agriculture, animals, medicine, humans, and the environment. By using its techniques, we can obtain genetically modified food products, human gene products, and therapeutically useful products.

## In Animals

Genetic engineering has produced **transgenic** animals, such as mice, rats, rabbits, pigs, sheep, and cows. These animals have been beneficial to the medical field by providing organs for transplants. Transgenic cows produce milk with extra nutrients. Some transgenic animals can also be beneficial for manufacturing certain products.

## Gene Therapy

Gene therapy is an experimental technique that uses genes to treat or prevent a disease, especially a hereditary disease. In this therapy, scientists supply copies of healthy genes to cells with variant or missing genes so that they can work properly.

## Humulin

In 1982, a drug called Humulin became the first genetically engineered drug approved by the U.S. Food and Drug Administration. It is used by millions of patients around the world every day for managing **diabetes**. Scientists cloned the gene for human insulin and created this drug.

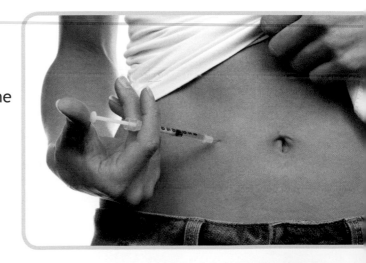

# Oil-eating Bacteria

Oil spills are serious dangers to wildlife and the environment, and cleaning them is a difficult task. The most well-known "oil-eating bacteria" is the genetically engineered form of bacterium under the genus *Psuedomonas*. It was developed by the microbiologist Ananda Mohan Chakrabarty.

# Medicine

In medicine, genetic engineering has been used to produce a variety of vaccines, antibodies, and vitamins. They have helped to control many diseases. Chemotherapy and radiology used by doctors in terminal diseases are also a gift of genetic research.

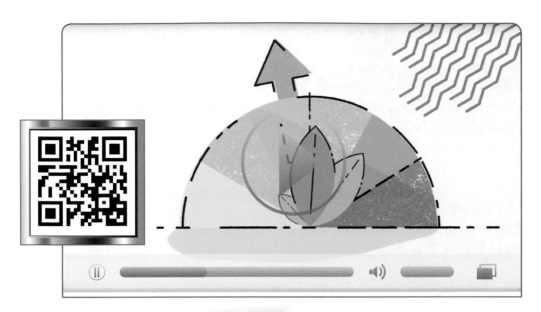

This video shows the process of genetic modification.

## SIDEBAR: DID YOU KNOW?

- In 1974, the scientist Rudolph Jaenisch created the first genetically engineered animal—a mouse.

- The Flavr-Savr tomato was the first genetically engineered food product. It went on the U.S. market in 1994, but was only available for three years.

# CLONING

A clone is defined as a number of identical molecules (genes), cells, or even organisms, all necessarily derived from a common ancestor. They are the carbon copies of a single parent. The process of producing genetically similar entities (genes, cells, and organisms) from a common ancestor by the mode of asexual reproduction is called cloning.

## Gene Cloning

Cloning refers to the synthesis of a large population of a single desired DNA fragment. Gene cloning is important in the fields of medicine (for example, in creating insulin) and agriculture (in food production). The various clones representing all the genes of an organism form the "gene library"

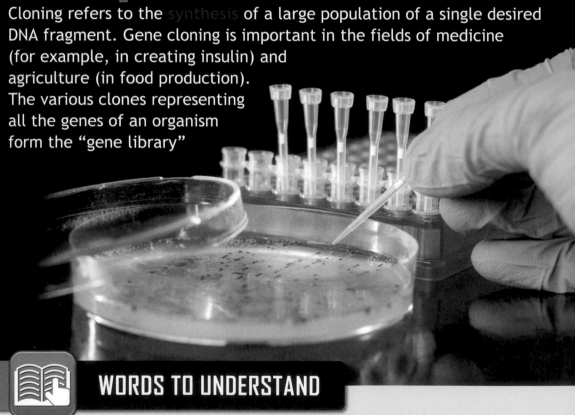

## WORDS TO UNDERSTAND

**morphologically:** referring to the structure and shape of an organism.
**physiologically:** referring to the functions of an organism.
**recombinant:** here, describes something (such as a cell or DNA strand) created by the combination of genetic material from separate sources.
**synthesis:** here, the creation of something, such as DNA fragments.

of that organism. From the gene library, a clone having a specific gene can be identified and multiplied for use.

# Cell Cloning

Cell cloning is the process of the formation of identical and multiple copies of the same cell. Clone cells are not only **morphologically** and **physiologically** identical, but also genetically identical. Cell cloning is chiefly required to multiply **recombinant** cells specified for the production of certain biochemicals, such as proteins, hormones, insulin, etc. The cloning process of unicellular organisms is simpler than that of multicellular organisms.

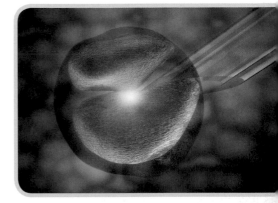

# Microbial Cloning

Several improved, genetically changed strains of microorganisms have been cloned for different applications, for example, *Escherichia coli* for the production of human insulin, *Bacillus thuringiensis* for Bt toxin, and so on.

# Importance of Cloning

Genetically engineered pigs can be cloned for organ transplantation in humans. Populations of endangered and rare animals and plants can also be increased by cloning. The improved varieties and breeds can be mass multiplied by this process. Moreover, the process of cloning need not wait for the favorable season; mass multiplication (cloning) of ornamental plants (roses, orchids) can be done year-round.

## Gene Cloning

This refers to the synthesis of a large population of a single desired DNA fragment. Gene cloning is important in the fields of medicine (insulin synthesis), agriculture (increase food production), and is also used for treating defective genes in humans. The various clones representing all the genes of an organism form the "gene library" of that organism. From the gene library, a clone having a specific gene can be identified and multiplied for use.

## Animal and Plant Cloning

Many plants have been cloned because of their medicinal or ornamental value. Cloning helps in their rapid production, while also making them virus-free or disease-resistant. On the other hand, formation of one or more genetically modified animals is called animal cloning. In recent years, a small number of firms have sprung up offering cloning services

for dog owners, so that beloved pets can "live again." However, it's important to understand that the clone of a pet is really only as similar to the original as an identical twin would be. After all, identical twins (also called monozygotic twins) are natural clones to each other; they develop from a single zygote by the splitting of the early embryo. Even a clone of your dog is not a literal copy of your dog—it is more like the dog's long-lost twin brother or sister.

Dolly the Sheep

## SIDEBAR: DID YOU KNOW?

- **Recombivax HB, the first genetically engineered human vaccine, has come into use to prevent hepatitis B.**
- **A sheep named Dolly was the world's first cloned mammal.**

# GENETICALLY MODIFIED ORGANISMS

Genetically modified organisms (GMOs) are created for human and animal consumption. Genetic engineering enables a desired trait to be enhanced in plants very rapidly and with great accuracy. Today, more than 90 percent of the corn and soybeans grown by farmers is genetically engineered in some way.

## WORDS TO UNDERSTAND

**molecular biology:** the branch of biology that studies the structure and function of macromolecules like proteins and nucleic acids essential to life.

**retrovirus:** a type of virus that reproduces by inserting a copy of its DNA into the host.

**salinity:** describes the level of salts in water.

**toxins:** poisonous substances.

# Why Genetically Modified Crops?

Plant geneticists isolate a gene responsible for a desirable trait in an organism and insert it into a plant. It is not necessary that the gene transferred in a plant should come from a plant source; the gene from nonplant organisms can also be used. For example, scientists have used the genes of *Bacillus thuringiensis*—bacteria that produce crystal proteins toxic to insect larvae—in corn and other crops to protect them against insects. The crystal protein gene enables crops to create their own fighting mechanism against insects.

# Other Benefits

Plants producing **toxins** selective against caterpillar larvae reduce the need for chemical sprays by 60 percent. This controls pollution of soil and waterways with chemicals while also sparing useful insects. Soil and groundwater pollution continues to be a problem in all parts of the world. Plants such as poplar trees have been genetically engineered to clean up heavy metal pollution from contaminated soil.

A gentically modified plum pox resistant variety of plum

# Adequate Supply of Food

The world population has crossed well over seven billion and is predicted to pass 11 billion by the year 2100. One of the biggest challenges will be ensuring an adequate food supply for our present and future population. Environmental factors beyond human control cause huge crop failures worldwide every year. Genetic engineering has the potential to avoid these losses by increasing the resistance of crops against **salinity**, cold, droughts, and other environmental extremities.

# Edible Vaccines for Good Health

Some crops can genetically engineered to contain additional vitamins and minerals, which can help in alleviating nutrient deficiencies. Medicines and vaccines are costly to produce and often require special storage conditions. Researchers are working to develop edible vaccines for various diseases, such as measles, cholera, and others. These vaccines will be much easier to store and administer than traditional vaccines.

## Examples of Genetically Modified Plants

| Genetically-conferred Trait | Example Organism |
|---|---|
| Herbicide tolerance | Soybean |
| Insect resistance | Corn |
| Altered fatty acid composition | Canola |
| Virus resistance | Plum |
| Vitamin enrichment | Rice |
| Vaccines | Tobacco |
| Oral vaccines | Maize |
| Faster maturation | Coho salmon |

While genetically engineered crops are present worldwide, genetically modified animals (known as transgenic animals) are still in their early stages of development. The main reason is that genetic engineering of animals is a slow and tedious process. It's also very expensive to accomplish. To modify an animal genetically, the new gene construct (known as transgene) must be inserted into the DNA of the host cell. There are a number of ways to do so.

# Microinjection

Microinjection means the direct injection of a foreign gene into a fertilized egg, which is randomly put into a female animal. This female animal acts as a surrogate mother for the egg.

## Viruses

Viruses, particularly **retroviruses**, are often used as "vectors" to introduce new genetic material into cells. A retrovirus is a virus that attaches to an organism's DNA and changes it to include a new characteristic.

## Embryonic Stem Cell Culture and Modification

Stem cells from embryos can turn into any type of cells, such as live cells, or skin cells. These cells are self-sustaining. Scientists modify these cells and add them to an embryo for the treatment of life-threatening diseases.

## Sperm-Mediated Transfer

This method uses a genetically modified sperm as a vector for introducing foreign DNA into the egg.

### TRANSGENIC MICE

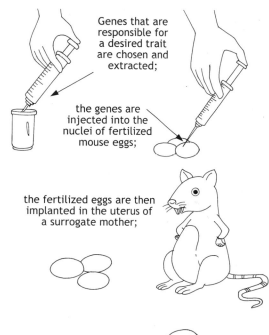

Genes that are responsible for a desired trait are chosen and extracted;

the genes are injected into the nuclei of fertilized mouse eggs;

the fertilized eggs are then implanted in the uterus of a surrogate mother;

the desired trait should be expressed by at least some of the offspring.

## Top Five Eccentric Transgenic Animals

• **GloFish:** GloFish was the first transgenic animal to be commercially available as a pet in the US and parts of Asia. It is a natural zebrafish which has fluorescent proteins extracted from jellyfish inserted into their DNA to make them glow green, orange, or red.

• **Brainbow Mouse:** Scientists at Harvard University have developed a special mouse using a genetic technique that utilizes four fluorescent proteins in varying combinations and saturations. It is called Brainbow mouse because they have individually labeled hundreds of nerve cells in its brain with 90 different color combinations.

- **Spider Goat:** Randy Lewis, molecular biologist and professor at University of Wyoming, has genetically modified goats and inserted spider silk gene into their DNA. These goats produce milk with silk protein which can be extracted and used to create spider silk, which is stronger than steel.

- **Cancer-resistant Mouse:** Researchers from the University of Kentucky have engineered a cancer-resistant mouse. This is due to the insertion of a gene into the mouse that codes for a protein called Par-4. This protein kills cancer cells without affecting normal cells.

- **Mighty Mouse:** Dr. Richard Hanson at Case Western Reserve University has created a mouse that can live longer and can run 25 times more than normal mice at the same speed. The mouse is genetically engineered to overproduce a metabolic enzyme, PEPCK-C, which assists the generation of glucose.

# Prospective Benefits

Scientists are producing genetically engineered animals for a variety of applications, including the production of pharmaceuticals and as a source of cells, tissues, and organs that can be transplanted into humans without rejection. Genetically engineered animals with traits for disease resistance and climatic tolerance may lead to the production of higher-quality food in those regions where diseases and climatic conditions limit the ability to raise food animals. Some GE (genetically engineered) animals may produce high-value industrial and consumer products.

## SIDEBAR: DID YOU KNOW?

- Genetically engineered animals were first developed in the 1980s.

- Scientists have created Golden rice, a GMO rich in vitamin A, to combat the deficiency of Vitamin A in developing countries where rice is the staple food.

# SOLVING CRIMES

People have used fingerprints in business transactions and legal affairs since ancient times. Archaeologists have discovered prehistoric clay tablets and seals with finger impressions that were used in ancient Babylon and China. The first-known observation that no two fingerprints are identical was made by a Persian doctor in the 14th century.

## William James Herschel

The first use of fingerprints in modern times was by William Herschel in 1858. Herschel was an officer in one of the provinces of British India. He took palm prints of locals to use in business contracts. Herschel believed that the palm prints bound people to their commitment more than signatures. As the practice grew, Herschel stopped asking for palm prints and let people give their fingerprints.

## First Crime Solved

The uniqueness of fingerprints was not established until much later in the 1880s. A British **anthropologist**, Sir Francis Galton, was one of the

 **WORDS TO UNDERSTAND**

**anthropologist:** someone who specializes in the scientific study of the origin, behavior, physical, social, and cultural development of humans.
**conventional:** here, describes something traditional or expected.
**radioactive:** emitting or relating to emission of ionizing radiation or particles.

first to observe that fingerprints could be used as a means of identification. In 1892, Juan Vucetich, an Argentine police official, was the first to solve a crime using fingerprints.

# What is DNA Fingerprinting?

Science has come a long way since the uniqueness of fingerprints was discovered. Instead of fingerprints investigators now use a much-advanced technique known as DNA fingerprinting to identify individuals. DNA fingerprints can be found using a minute tissue or a few cells such as roots of hairs, or nuclei of blood. Unlike **conventional** fingerprints, the DNA fingerprint is the same for every cell, tissue, and organ of a person.

## Process of DNA Fingerprinting

Scientists cut the long strands of DNA obtained from tissue evidence into smaller segments using various chemicals. Each segment has the same repeating sequence of bases (or nucleotides). The fragments are then separated using a process known as gel electrophoresis, and the separated fragments are copied on a nylon paper. Next, a set of **radioactive** probes is introduced to the sample. These probes are synthetic segments of DNA of the same length as the sample, with bases that complement the code, and bind to it. Suppose the sample segment has the sequence ATCATCATCATCATC, the introduced probe would have the complementary code TAGTAGTAGTAGTAG. An X-ray film is exposed to the nylon paper to mark the places where the radioactive probes are bound to the DNA fragments. The dark bands on X-ray film represent the DNA fingerprints.

## Uses of DNA Fingerprinting

Over the last decade, DNA fingerprinting, and scientists who can identify the remains of dead people and animals, have helped investigators solve cases with little evidence. It has also helped people find their lost children. DNA fingerprinting has been successfully used to study the breeding pattern of animals and plants.

1 Extraction

DNA sample

2 Restriction enzymes

3 Electrophoresis

long DNA fragments

short DNA fragments

4 Transfer to membrane

5 Incubation with labelled probes

6 X-ray

DNA fingerprint

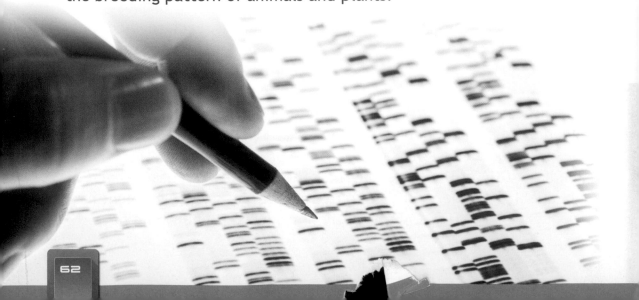

# Results

In the case of crime investigation, DNA samples from suspects are collected and subjected to the same procedure. The dark band on the X-ray film (i.e., the DNA fingerprints), as observed in the above case, will be same as that of the accused. Similarly, the DNA fingerprints of children can be compared with those of their parents in the case of disputed-parentage cases.

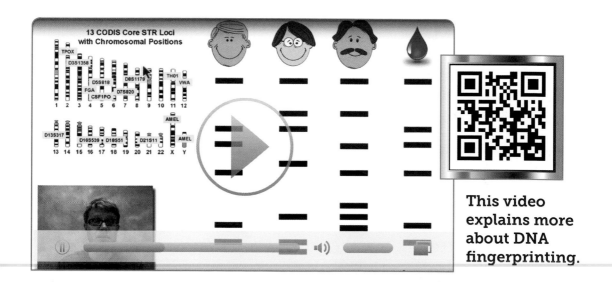

This video explains more about DNA fingerprinting.

## SIDEBAR: DID YOU KNOW?

- Sir Alec Jeffreys invented the technique of DNA fingerprinting in 1984.
- DNA fingerprinting is also known as DNA profiling.

# GENETIC MEDICINE

Genetic engineering has many promising applications in the field of medicine. Researchers are using it to diagnose and predict diseases and develop drugs to treat serious illnesses like cancer, Alzheimer's, diabetes, and cystic fibrosis. From vaccines in bananas to genetically engineered transplant organs, genetic engineering is expected to alter conventional medicine in a variety of important ways.

## Vaccines

A vast number of vaccines are now developed commercially using DNA technology. Previously, vaccines were made by **denaturing** the disease-causing organism and injecting it into humans. Unfortunately, the patient still sometimes ended up with the disease. However, in DNA technology, only the outside shell of the microorganism is copied and injected into a harmless host to create the vaccine.

## WORDS TO UNDERSTAND

**denaturing:** altering or modifying something so that all its original qualities are removed.

**gene therapy:** transplanting genes into cells to replace missing or damaged genes; used to reverse genetic disorders.

**predictive:** describes something that can be used to forecast what may happen in the future.

This method is comparatively safer because the actual disease-causing microorganism is not transferred to the host. The immune system is activated by specific proteins on the surface of the  microorganism.

## Common Genetically Engineered Vaccines

- Most influenza vaccines
- Rabies vaccines given to pets
- The West Nile vaccine given to horses
- Hepatitis B
- Hepatitis A
- Chicken pox

## The Potential for Edible Vaccines

One day children may get immunized by eating foods instead of enduring shots. Research done on potatoes shows that genes can be put successfully into potato plants to make vaccines against cholera, diarrhea, and hepatitis B. Scientists are also planning to genetically engineer bananas, tomatoes, and corn to have vaccines in them. These would then be grown in developing countries where diseases such as cholera and diarrhea are very common. Edible vaccines are still in the experimental phase.

## Antibiotics

Genetic engineering can be used to produce antibiotics on a large scale by getting a certain desirable chemical from an organism and inserting the gene that codes for that chemical into a bacterium such as *E. coli*. Since bacteria reproduce very quickly, scientists would have enough chemical to harvest and sell as a drug within a very short period.

# Xenotransplantation

Xenotransplantation is the process of taking an organ from a certain species and transplanting it into another species. Genetically engineered pigs may someday overcome the severe donor organ shortage that leads to the death of hundreds of thousands of patients every year. Scientists are working on pigs to eliminate a gene called the gal-transferase gene from their bodies because this gene is rejected by human bodies. A few more human genes will also be added to make the pig tissue more acceptable to our immune system.

# Predictive Medicine and Gene Therapy

**Predictive** medicine involves using genetics to predict the probability of future disease in an individual so he can be proactive in implementing lifestyle modifications and getting regular medical checkups. By isolating and studying the genetic structure of cells from unborn babies, scientists can detect diseases which the babies may later have. Some genetic diseases occur because certain genes are missing or do not work properly. Replacing the disease-causing genes with normal ones via **gene therapy** can help to cure problems like cystic fibrosis, cancer, and various liver diseases.

## SIDEBAR: DID YOU KNOW?

- Human growth hormone, which corrects a form of dwarfism and helps to heal wounds, is produced by genetically engineered bacteria and yeasts.

- Scientists believe more than 4,000 diseases result from mutated genes inherited from one's parents.

# FAMOUS GENETICISTS

Mendel's studies in genetics have been carried forward by later generations of geneticists. The progress and advancement of genetics owes to the work of many who dedicated their lives to the task.

## Thomas Hunt Morgan

Thomas Hunt Morgan was an American evolutionary biologist, geneticist, and embryologist who discovered the role played by chromosomes in heredity. His experiments at his famous "fly lab" (at Columbia University, New York) where he collected **Drosophila** mutants led to the discovery. He studied white mutation and sex-linked inheritance, which provided the first evidence that chromosomes are carriers of genetic material. Further studies conducted by him led to the discovery of recombination and the first genetic maps. His discoveries formed the basis of the modern science of genetics. He won a Nobel Prize in 1933 for his work.

 **WORDS TO UNDERSTAND**

**biochemist:** someone who specializes in the branch of science concerned with the chemical and physiochemical processes occurring within living organisms.

**Drosophila:** common house fly.

**immunochemistry:** a branch of biochemistry concerned with immune responses and systems.

# Har Gobind Khorana

Har Gobind Khorana was an Indian-born U.S **biochemist**. With his team of two (Marshall Warren Nirenberg and Robert William Holley), Khorana showed how the genetic components of a cell's nucleus control the synthesis of proteins. His biggest contribution was the first synthesis of an artificial yeast gene and its successful functional expression in *E. coli* in 1979. In the 1980s, he synthesized the gene for rhodopsin (a protein involved in vision). Khorana's contributions have played a significant role in the development of the biotechnology industry.

# Oswald Avery

Oswald Avery was a Canadian-born American biologist and a pioneer in **immunochemistry**. He is best known for his discovery in 1944, with his coworkers Colin MacLeod and Maclyn McCarty, that genes and chromosomes are made of DNA. The three of them discovered the "transforming principle" that DNA is an active ingredient in genetic transformation—the agent of change in all living beings. Prior to this, it was believed that proteins were the agents of genetic transformation.

# Mahlon Hoagland

Mahlon Hoagland was a U.S. physician and biochemist who co-discovered transfer RNA and the mechanisms behind amino acid activation. It revealed how DNA is translated into the proteins that carry out its genetic instructions. This led to the discovery of tRNA, which transports amino acids to messenger RNA.

## Martha Chase

Martha Chase was an American geneticist who, in collaboration with Alfred Hershey, experimentally proved Avery's transforming principle in 1952. Hershey and Chase's experiments with bacteriophage (a virus that specifically infects bacterial cells) convinced everyone that DNA was the genetic material.

## Linus Pauling

Linus Pauling was an American biochemist and one of the most influential chemists in history. He won a Nobel Prize in 1954 for his research into the nature of the chemical bond, the structure of molecules and crystals, and the application of the resulting concepts to explain the structure proteins. He was the first to construct the alpha-helical structure of a protein. He developed the theory of complementarity and used it to explain how genes might act as templates for the formation of enzymes. He played a supporting role in James Watson's and Francis Crick's discovery of the double helix structure of DNA.

 **SIDEBAR: DID YOU KNOW?**

- Thomas Hunt Morgan's wife, Lilian Vaughan Sampson, contributed significantly to his *Drosophila* experiments.
- Linus Pauling is often regarded as the founding father of molecular biology.

# POTENTIAL DOWNSIDES OF GENETIC ENGINEERING

Genetic engineering is an emerging field and we can't always predict what might result from putting the DNA of one species into another. Scientists have identified several potentially harmful effects of genetically modified organisms on the environment and human health. In addition to the known risks, genetic engineering may also pose risks that scientists have not been able to assess due to an incomplete understanding of physiology, genetics, and nutrition.

## Allergic Reactions

There is potential for genetically engineered foods to cause known and unknown allergies. For example, if genes from nuts are inserted into other foods, it could provoke severe reactions in people with nut allergies. Genetically engineered foods also have the possibility of creating new allergies. The new combinations of genes and traits have the potential to create allergic reactions that have never existed before.

FOOD ALLERGY

 **WORDS TO UNDERSTAND**

**abnormality:** an irregularity or malformation.

**pathogens:** microorganisms that can cause disease.

**pesticide:** a substance used for destroying insects or other organisms harmful for plants.

**transparency:** openness.

# Gene Mutation

Scientists are not sure whether the insertion of foreign DNA into an organism could destabilize it and encourage **abnormalities**. There is a possibility that a new gene might trigger some original gene in the engineered plant or animal to mutate and change.

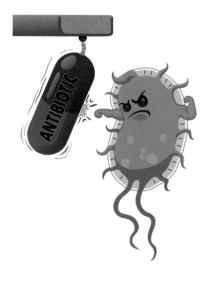

# Antibiotic Resistance

There is potential for genetically engineered food to make disease-causing bacteria even more resistant to **antibiotics**, thereby increasing the spread of diseases throughout the world. Most genetically engineered plant foods carry antibiotic-resistant genes. The concern is that eating these foods may reduce the ability of antibiotics to fight diseases. The resistant genes might be transferred to human or animal **pathogens**, making them immune to antibiotics.

# Damage to the Environment

A big concern is whether genetically modified organisms can spread, passing their foreign genes to wild species. For example, GE crops can cross-pollinate with weeds and create super weeds that could become difficult to control. If GE fish escape from fish farms, they can upset the ecology of oceans and may cause the extinction of native species. Released GE bacteria and viruses could have even worse effects than plants and animals because they reproduce and mutate much faster. This will contaminate "non-GE environments" and create uncontrollable genetic pollution. GE crops often manufacture their own pesticides, which can result in more **pesticides** in our food.

# Randomness and Genetic Engineering

Though we would like to believe that genetic modification is a completely precise technology, that is not necessarily the case.

A gene can be cut out precisely from the DNA of an organism but its insertion into the DNA of another organism is entirely random. It might disrupt the order of the genes on the chromosome and result in unexpected changes in the functioning of the cells. Existing molecules may be manufactured in inaccurate quantities or new molecules may be produced. Products made with GMOs do have the potential to carry unexpected toxins that could be dangerous.

## Challenges for Farmers

Seeds of genetically engineered crops are more expensive than those of conventional crops. Some insurance companies are hesitant to insure the crops because of the associated risks. Farmers growing genetically engineered crops have to sign obligatory contracts with the biotechnology producers which ask them to use only the herbicides produced by that company. These contracts also prohibit them from the traditional practice of saving seed for the next season.

## Labeling and GMOs

Currently, most foods containing genetically engineered ingredients sold in the US markets are not labeled. Consumers have no way of finding out whether the food they are buying contains GE ingredients or not. The food products containing soya flour, soya oil, canola oil, and corn extracts are most likely to contain GE ingredients.  In 2016, the U.S. Congress passed a law that requires food companies to disclose if there are GMOs included in their products.  However, this information will be included in a QR code on the package, so that consumers can get the information by scanning the code with their phones.  Advocates for **transparency** in food labeling are still pushing to get more obviously visible information about GMOs included right on the labels.

## Global Opinions on GMOs

Around 50 countries of the world, including Australia, Japan, and all the countries in the European Union, have put restrictions on the production and sale of GE organisms. Many international organizations like the Food and Agriculture Organization (FAO), the World Health Organization (WHO), and the United States Food and Drug Administration (FDA) have issued guidelines for the safety assessment of GE organisms and products derived from them.

## Are All GMOs Bad?

Contrary to some assumptions, engineered organisms released into the environment are not likely to proliferate. Likewise, all genetically engineered foods are not toxic. They are simply new to our system and contain proteins we have never eaten before.

That said, certain engineered organisms may be harmful due to the novel gene combinations used to engineer them. The risks of genetically engineered organisms must be assessed case by case, since these risks can differ greatly from one genetic combination to another.

Do you know whats in your food?

 SIDEBAR: DID YOU KNOW?

- For commercial reasons, most food products containing GMOs are not labeled despite the presence of labeling laws in certain countries.

- Transgenic foods may mislead consumers by appearing fresh when they are not. For example, a bright red, genetically engineered tomato could be several weeks old.

# TEXT-DEPENDENT QUESTIONS

1. Why do people in the same family often look similar?

2. What did Pythagoras believe about heredity?

3. Who was Gregor Mendel?

4. What is the theory of natural selection? What are its main points?

5. What are chromosomes? How many do humans have?

6. What are alleles?

7. How do genetic mutations occur?

8. What is the cell cycle? How does it work?

9. What are some of the key uses of genetic engineering?

10. What are some of the possible problems with genetic engineering?

# RESEARCH PROJECTS

1. Read the chapter in this book about the cell cycle and find additional sources that explain it. Using those sources, create a poster with illustrations that show the different stages, including the interphase and mitosis.

2. Select one of the genetic conditions discussed in this book and find out more about it. What are the symptoms? What can doctors do to help people with that condition? Write a pamphlet to explain the condition and what people can do to manage the situation.

3. Choose one of the many scientists discussed in the book for further study. Options include Gregor Mendel, Jean-Baptiste Lamarck, Charles Darwin, or one of the more contemporary scientists discussed in the geneticists chapter. What kind of scientific background did the person have? What were his or her contributions to the field? How has his or her work impacted today's world?

4. Find out more about how DNA evidence is used in the criminal justice system. Imagine that you are a defense attorney, and write a list of different ways that you might use DNA evidence to prove your client's innocence.

5. Investigate the complex debates around the issue of genetically modified organisms (GMOs). Are they good or bad for farmers? For consumers? For the environment? Should GMO food products be labeled? Consider partnering with another student to have a debate—one of you should argue in favor of GMOs, and one against. Or you could study both sides yourself and write a list of pros on one side and cons on the other. Write an editorial that defends the position you think is correct.

# FURTHER READING

Burgan, Michael. *Food Engineering*. New York: Scholastic, 2015.

— — —. *Genetic Engineering*. New York: Scholastic, 2016.

Mooney, Carla. *Genetics: Breaking the Code of Your DNA*.  White River Junction, VT: Nomad Press, 2014.

Rooney, Anne. *Genetic Engineering*. New York: Crabtree Publishing, 2016.

# INTERNET RESOURCES

All About Genetics.
**https://kidshealth.org/en/parents/about-genetics.html**
This site from the Nemours Foundation contains clear explanations of topics related to heredity, genes, and genetics.

Genetic Literacy Project
**https://geneticliteracyproject.org/**
A not-for-profit organization that collects news and data about genetic research.

Genetics.
**https://kids.britannica.com/students/article/genetics/274516**
A thorough explanation of genetics and the history of genetics research, with many useful illustrations.

Just for Kids! A Cartoon Guide to Genetics
**https://history.nih.gov/exhibits/genetics/kids.htm**
An illustrated slideshow about how genes work from the National Institute of Health; includes a link with information for teachers.

# INDEX

# INDEX

proteins, 22, 28, 38–40
*Psiam sativum*, 12, 13*fig*
*Psuedomonas*, 48
Pythagoras, 9

## Q
QR Video
  cell cycle, 30
  chromosomes, 20
  DNA profiling, 63
  genetic modification, 49
  heredity and family traits, 11

## R
radiology, 48
ramets, 7
recessiveness, 24–26, 41
recombinant cells, 50–51
Recombivax HB, 53
red blood cells, 40
retroviruses, 54, 57
Rh factor, 41
ribosomal RNA (rRNA), 39
ribosomes, 38–39
RNA (ribonucleic acid), 7, 19, 28, 37–39
  compared to DNA, 37
  function of, 38
  structure, 37
  types of, 39

## S
Sampson, Lilian Vaughan, 69
segregation, 8, 13, 18
sexual reproduction, 7–8, 18
sickle cell anemia, 26, 45
species, 8, 11, 15
sperm, 8, 23, 31*fig*
sperm-mediated transfer, 57
spider goat, 58
stem cells, 57

## T
thalassemias, 45
Tijo, Joe Hin, 43
tissues, 27
trait transmission, 6–7, 9, 13, 18–19, 21–22, 24–26, 34–35
transcription, 39
transfer RNA (tRNA), 39, 68
transgenic animals, 56–59, 66, 73
transgenic organisms, 46–49, 73
transplantation, 47, 51, 66
Turner's syndrome, 43–44
twins, 53

## V
vaccines, 48, 56, 64–65
variation, 7–8, 12–13, 16, 71–72
Virchow, Rudolf, 30
viruses, 7, 37, 57
von Tschermak, Erich, 14
Vucetich, Juan, 61

## W
Watson, James, 69
white blood cells, 40
World Health Organization (WHO), 73

## X
xenotransplantation. *See* transplantation

## Z
zygote, 8, 18